Mother Teresa

Jennifer Strand

abdopublishing.com

Published by Abdo Zoom™, PO Box 398166, Minneapolis, Minnesota 55439. Copyright © 2017 by Abdo Consulting Group, Inc. International copyrights reserved in all countries. No part of this book may be reproduced in any form without written permission from the publisher. Abdo Zoom™ is a trademark and logo of Abdo Consulting Group, Inc.

Printed in the United States of America, North Mankato, Minnesota
072016
092016

Cover Photo: Bettmann/Corbis
Interior Photos: Bettmann/Corbis, 1; AP Images, 4, 11, 17; Jean-Claude Francolon/Gamma-Rapho/Getty Images, 5, 13; iStockphoto, 6; Keystone Features/Getty Images, 7; Shutterstock Images, 8–9; Steve Pyle/AP Images, 9; Three Lions/Stringer/Getty Images, 10; Saurabh Das/AP Images, 14; Henrik Laurvik/AP Images, 15; Biks Das/AP Images, 18–19

Editor: Brienna Rossiter
Series Designer: Madeline Berger
Art Direction: Dorothy Toth

Publisher's Cataloging-in-Publication Data
Names: Strand, Jennifer, author.
Title: Mother Teresa / by Jennifer Strand.
Description: Minneapolis, MN : Abdo Zoom, [2017] | Series: Great women |
    Includes bibliographical references and index.
Identifiers: LCCN 2016941353 | ISBN 9781680792232 (lib. bdg.) |
    ISBN 9781680793918 (ebook) | 9781680794809 (Read-to-me ebook)
Subjects: LCSH: Teresa, Mother, 1910-1997--Juvenile literature. | Missionaries of
    Charity--History--20th century--Biography--Juvenile literature.
Classification: DDC 271/.97 [B]--dc23
LC record available at http://lccn.loc.gov/2016941353

Table of Contents

Mother Teresa was
a **humanitarian**.

She helped
people who
were very poor.

Mother Teresa was born on August 26, 1910. She grew up in what is now Macedonia.

Her birth name was
Agnes Gonxha Bojaxhiu.

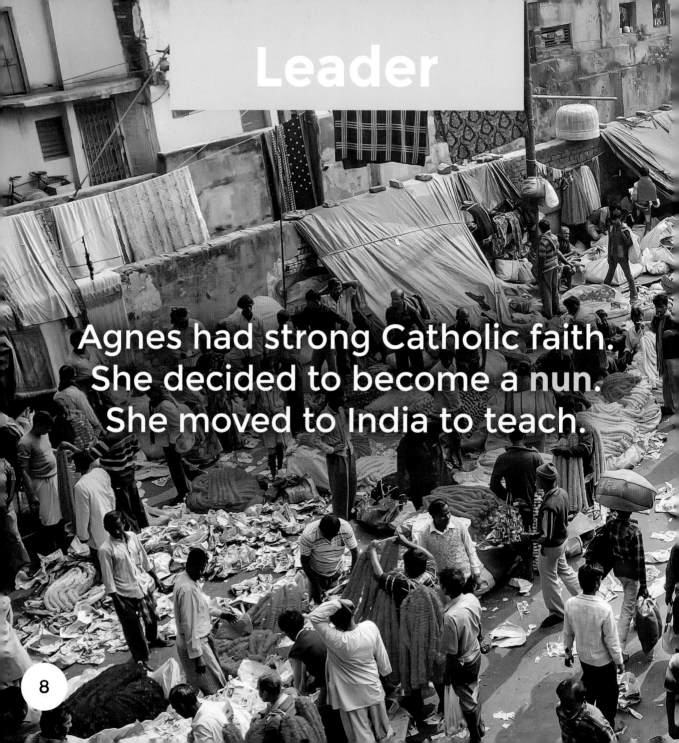

Leader

Agnes had strong Catholic faith.
She decided to become a nun.
She moved to India to teach.

Later she was called
Mother Teresa.

In India very poor people were not being cared for. Mother Teresa wanted to help.

She started a new **order**
of nuns. They cared for
sick people and **outcasts**.

Mother Teresa opened many homes. Some were for people who were dying. Others were for children. At the homes, nuns took care of people.

Mother Teresa's homes spread around the world.

In 1979 she won the **Nobel Prize** for peace.

Legacy

Mother Teresa traveled around the world. She helped people hurt by wars or disasters. World leaders asked her for advice.

She used her fame to help poor people.

She died on September 5, 1997. But her order still cares for the poor.

Mother Teresa

Born: August 26, 1910

Birthplace: Skopje, Ottoman Empire

Known For: Mother Teresa was a Catholic nun. She took care of very poor people.

Died: September 5, 1997

Key Dates

1910: Agnes Gonxha Bojaxhiu is born on August 26.

1928: Agnes trains to be a nun. She is later called Mother Teresa.

1952: Mother Teresa opens a home for people who are dying.

1979: Mother Teresa wins the Nobel Peace Prize.

1997: Mother Teresa dies on September 5.

2016: Mother Teresa is made a saint on September 4.

Glossary

humanitarian - a person who works to help other people have better lives.

Nobel Prize - an important award given out each year.

nun - a woman who belongs to a religious order.

order - a group of people living in a religious community.

outcast - someone who has been rejected by other people.

Booklinks

For more information
on **Mother Teresa**, please visit
booklinks.abdopublishing.com

Z**m** In on Biographies!

Learn even more with the Abdo Zoom
Biographies database. Check out
abdozoom.com for more information.

Index